IMAGES
of Aviation

McCONNELL AIR FORCE BASE

This is the iconic “first flight” image. With Orville Wright at the controls and Wilbur Wright running alongside at right, the Wright Flyer takes to the skies at Kitty Hawk, North Carolina, on December 17, 1903. The initial flight never rose any higher than 10 feet off the ground. (Courtesy U.S. Air Force Historical Research Institute.)

On the cover: An XB-47 executes a rocket assisted take-off (RATO) from the Wichita Air Force Base runway about 1951. The RATO system consisted of 18 rockets mounted into either side of the B-47 to add additional thrust. The B-47’s General Electric J-35 engines were underpowered when launching at near-maximum or maximum weight. (Courtesy Kansas Aviation Museum.)

IMAGES
of Aviation

McCONNELL AIR FORCE BASE

Steve A. Larsen

ARCADIA PUBLISHING

ISBN 978-0-7385-6183-7

Published by Arcadia Publishing
Charleston, South Carolina

Printed in the United States of America

Library of Congress Control Number: 2008927313

For all general information, please contact Arcadia Publishing:
Telephone 843-853-2070
Fax 843-853-0044
E-mail sales@arcadiapublishing.com
For customer service and orders:
Toll-Free 1-888-313-2665

Visit us on the Internet at www.arcadiapublishing.com

CONTENTS

ACKNOWLEDGMENTS

Books are never easy undertakings. Even modest efforts such as this take time, patience, and, above all, the assistance of many people. I would be remiss if I did not acknowledge those whose own efforts took this book from a notion in my head four years ago to a reality. My colleague Yancey Mailes, also a military historian, was the catalyst who motivated me in November 2007 from a notion to actually placing this project in motion. I owe him a debt of gratitude. The dedicated volunteers of the Kansas Aviation Museum who struggle against all odds to preserve Wichita's rich aviation history also deserve credit and great thanks, particularly the museum's intrepid archivist, Andy Lebowsky, a former B-47 navigator-bombardier. Andy and his team were first-rate professionals.

A colleague of mine, Mark Schock, deserves my gratitude for supplying photographs of his father and the base during its early years. I owe you big Mark, thanks. SMSgt. (retired) Ronald Dellapena also graciously donated images of the B-47 years from his own collection. I wish to express as well my deep thanks to him.

Many of the images in this book were shot by Public Affairs personnel over the decades. I specifically wish to thank the staff of the 22d Air Refueling Wing Office of Public Affairs. All of them on more than one occasion have served as "partners in crime" when accomplishing various sorts of history and heritage publications for both McConnell Air Force Base and the U.S. Air Force. This group of military professionals were also instrumental in clearing the hurdles so that the many images appearing here could even be put into a public work such as this.

This book is dedicated to two groups of people; first to Wichita's aviation pioneers whose dedication and vision established Wichita as the "Air Capital of the World," laying a foundation that made the city an ideal location for a U.S. Air Force mission. Second, I wish to acknowledge with deep respect the men and women past, present, and future of McConnell Air Force Base. Most of us are unable to truly understand the personal sacrifices these outstanding people make on our behalf. They made and make this history. This book is very much for them and about them.

INTRODUCTION

In June 1862, Brig. Gen. Fitz-John Porter climbed aboard an observation balloon named the *Intrepid* belonging to self-proclaimed "Professor" Thaddeus Lowe near Yorktown, Virginia, to have a look at Confederate activity. The balloon's gas bag was filled with hydrogen gas produced by pouring sulfuric acid over iron filings. Porter went up alone, and the tether meant to hold the balloon in place broke free from the ground. Porter was then on his own. As the balloon drifted over Confederate lines, Porter quite literally needed the intervention of divine providence to save him from capture, and he got it. The wind direction changed, and the balloon drifted back to safety among the Union lines. So ended one of the first uses of airpower in American military operations—an abortive attempt at what is now called intelligence, surveillance, and reconnaissance, or ISR. In Porter's day and for a long time thereafter it was simply called "observation." While Wichita did not perhaps launch its bid into aviation in such a precarious manner, it nonetheless was built by men as colorful as Porter and Lowe.

Wichita might well appear to be a natural fit for the aviation industry from our modern perception. Many assume the central location, the wind, or the flat lands hold the keys to this city's far-reaching aviation footprint. It was not the central location, flat topography, or generally favorable winds. Oil created aviation here; specifically, the money oil brought to one man. Jake Mollendick's single-minded stubbornness made the aircraft industry possible here. Through his efforts, pioneers of aviation's "golden age," Matty Laird and Lloyd Stearman both came to Wichita. Walter Beech, a former army-enlisted pilot, was already here and also worked with Mollendick and Laird. Clyde Cessna, who came from Iowa, began flying his Silverwing airplane first on the Oklahoma salt flats in 1911, less than 10 years after the Wright brothers' seminal flight, also came to Wichita to build and sell airplanes.

How U.S. Air Force bases come to be what they are and where they are located is a complex question that does not offer an easy answer. U.S. Air Force members have long cheekily joked that the common methodology used to site and place U.S. Air Force bases boiled down to a relatively simple thing: the senior leadership looks for a golf course then builds a base around it. This is certainly an amusing response to the question though not the correct one. The actual rationale employed changes with the times and the service's mission requirements. When one adds in the political push and shove that occurs within the halls of the U.S. Capitol building, then everything becomes all the more murky. While some bases often maintain the same basic mission year in and year out from their founding, such as Langley Air Force Base and its assignment of pursuit and fighter aircraft, others like McConnell Air Force Base take on a more evolutionary development and frequent mission changes as determined by the nation's strategic defense needs.

The history, creation, and further evolution of McConnell Air Force Base provides a glimpse into how sometimes the political push and shove is a secondary concern. Wichita as a community is aviation. All apologies to Dayton and Kitty Hawk, but American aviation was indeed largely born in what was, for the time, a relatively insignificant town better known for cowboys and gunslingers. The city's economy had been tied to the cattle industry, but by the start of the 20th century, railroads made Wichita largely irrelevant where such bovine activity was concerned. The city's economy needed a boost and that boost came from aviation. The aircraft industry in fact spans more years of Wichita's history than cowboys and cattle drives ever did. The era of the cowboy was a relatively short-lived one. Wichita is not the "Old Cowtown," but it is very much the "Old Airtown."

Originally a hay field that was then six miles southeast of Wichita, the "California Section" was a mere slip of land at 600 acres compared to the roughly 2,600 acres that now comprise McConnell Air Force Base. Wichita realized its first aviation extravaganza at a fair, the Peerless Prophets' Jubilee, in 1908, a mere five years after the Wright brothers' first flight. The fair was to feature a dirigible flight by Frank Goodale, a gentleman billed back east as "the world's youngest boy aeronaut." He was 19 years old at the time of the Wichita event. Goodale was to fly a Knabenshue airship over the city but nothing resulted except several aborted attempts stopped by the notorious Kansas wind. Wichita's first aerial demonstration ended for naught. That same year, the U.S. Army Signal Corps began soliciting bids for their first military aircraft. U.S. Army Signal Corps Aeroplane No. 1 would eventually be a Wright B model aircraft and based at Fort Sam Houston. It was in 1924 when the California Section realized its point of no return and the parcel's years as an insignificant hay field and ersatz flying field came to an end.

The National Air Congress of 1924 was the single largest air meet held in the United States that year outside of the well-established International Air Races held at Wright Field (now, Wright-Patterson Air Force Base) in Dayton. These races were in large part an attempt to first put Wichita into the national spotlight where aviation was concerned and second to drum up support of the local citizenry. The local chapter members of the National Aeronautic Association were determined to see a major airfield constructed to service transcontinental air travel as no passenger conveyance or airmail plane in the country flew non-stop coast-to-coast.

The success of the meet drove construction of the terminal building on the California Section. With ground broken in 1929 and after a construction slow-down produced by the crash of the New York Stock Exchange that same year, the terminal building opened its doors in 1935. By 1948, the Wichita Municipal Airport was the second busiest terminal in the United States averaging 30 flights per day and over 10,000 operations per year. While commercial aviation began its development in the first decade of the 20th century and the early 1920s with aircraft companies like Swallow and Travel Air, military aircraft construction took on a life of its own during the World War II era. The Boeing plant on South Oliver Street (formerly the Stearman Aircraft Company) began producing all manner of U.S. Air Force aircraft. Even at this early point, a strong advocacy existed in the city for a military air presence. A number of city officials and local dignitaries traveled to the state capital to directly lobby the governor and adjutant general to base the National Guard's air arm in Wichita as early as 1940. While the Air Force Material Command had a number of procurement officials in town, chiefly at the Boeing plant, the establishment and activation of the 127th Observation Squadron of the Kansas Air National Guard created Wichita's first permanent U.S. Air Force presence. Formal recognition required that the unit hold at least 103 airmen on their rolls. This occurred officially on August 4, 1941, when the adjutant general's inspection verified the unit possessed 110 personnel.

The World War II era marked a period of robust local aircraft manufacturing for the U.S. Army Air Force with Boeing, Beech, and Cessna all manufacturing aircraft destined for war service. Among the airframes produced locally were Cessna's UC-78 transport aircraft, the Beechcraft AT-11, the now venerable Stearman Kaydet trainer, by then a Boeing product, and this latter company's now legendary B-29 Superfortress. All three of these companies also produced CG-4A Jayhawk gliders used heavily alongside the British-built Horsa glider in the Normandy

Invasion. The B-29 program alone resulted in the construction of two federal housing districts, Hilltop Manor and the appropriately named Planeview, just outside the airport's confines to accommodate the large influx of Boeing employees brought in to manufacture U.S. Air Force bombers.

With the close of World War II, there was little doubt that the U.S. Air Force presence was in Wichita to stay. The Air National Guard continued their mission, as did the Air Force Materiel Command's procurement operation with Boeing closing down the B-29 production line but quickly gaining a new contract for production of the B-47. A mere six years after war's end, the regular U.S. Air Force arrived to open up a major combat crew training wing at the Wichita Municipal Airport, which also spurred construction of Mid-Continent Airport on the west side of the city. With the arrival of Col. Henry "H. R." Spicer in April 1951, the active duty U.S. Air Force began operations that continued through numerous mission changes and to the present era with the 22d Air Refueling Wing.

In the course of McConnell Air Force Base's history, two central themes exist. First is the strong commitment of the city of Wichita to aviation and its support to the local U.S. Air Force community. Whether it was through the early advocates of "aeroplane" manufacture and the aviation industry who pursued military applications locally or the aggressive post-war pursuit of Air Force basing at the municipal airport and continued support ever since, Wichita almost seemingly possessed a destiny for a strong Air Force presence. Second, the U.S. Air Force itself, from its inception first as a subordinate organization within the U.S. Army and later as an independent service, established a posture and later a legacy for evolution and a forward look that remained more adaptable and malleable than its more tradition-bound sister services.

The history of McConnell Air Force Base embodies this evolutionary tradition. Beginning with the revolutionary-for-its-time B-47 Stratojet then moving into the space age when taking up the Titan II missile program, while simultaneously housing first tactical fighter wings and later a B-1 bomber wing, all of which were later followed by KC-135 Stratotankers, airmen at McConnell Air Force Base and the citizens of Wichita witnessed a seemingly continuous stream of changes. There were 14 different weapon systems, 4 different major commands, and 9 different primary missions in a rather brief 57 years, with each organization leaving its own lasting changes to the physical structure of the base that contributed to its evolution from a Cold War bomber training site to what is now considered the U.S. Air Force's "Center For Air Refueling Excellence." These changes did not just limit themselves to the active U.S. Air Force. The 184th Intelligence Wing of the Kansas Air National Guard also experienced a number of mission changes over the years that began humbly enough with a single observation squadron that later evolved into a fighter group, only to then assume the role of a B-1 bomber wing, followed by a refueling mission, to its new mission as an intelligence unit that fundamentally and directly supports ongoing operations in Southwest Asia. In a very real sense, Wichita was and is a city meant for aviation, not the least of which is military aviation. Through the ensuing chapters and photographs, this book illustrates how McConnell Air Force Base developed from its early years to become the 21st century military operation it is today.

The beginning of this story then lies with Wichita's aviation pioneers and their development of a true "Air Capital" and later the symbiotic advantages left available to first the U.S. Department of War and later the U.S. Department of Defense for a strong national-local relationship. This is above all a story of evolution. Moving from what was little more than pasture land to the busiest air refueling operation in the U.S. Air Force, McConnell Air Force Base is also a story of people, civilian and military, and the benefit obtained through mutual trust, respect, and admiration. The history of McConnell Air Force Base stands as a testament to what men and women who possess vision and the persistence to see such vision through can accomplish. This book is very much their story from humble, promising beginnings until the present day.

Seen here is the Army of the Potomac's ersatz balloonist Brig. Gen. Fitz-John Porter. He was one of the first military leaders to realize the potential of aviation as a military application. (Courtesy Library of Congress.)

One

From Modest Beginnings to National Defense 1920–1962

McConnell Air Force Base came into being in what one might consider a completely unrelated footnote to local history. A West Point cadet named J. Earl Schaefer rather cheekily annotated three choices on his career "dream sheet" for the U.S. Army. Schaefer wrote down, "Aviation, aviation, aviation." How did this response effect the development of what became McConnell Air Force Base? After all, this inauspicious event on the part of one passionate cadet happened in 1917. A mere 14 years after the Wright brothers made that first fateful flight in Kitty Hawk.

Two things are important in this anecdote. Schaefer loved airplanes. Second he was from Wichita. He never lost sight of this and became, after his U.S. Army service, a man determined to establish Wichita as a center for aircraft. He and several associates, chief among them L. W. Clapp, laid the ground work for establishing a very important mid-continent hub for air travel known then as the Wichita Municipal Airport. That a military application would arrive a mere six years after the airport's opening was not a monumental surprise. Even at the time of the National Air Congress in 1924, an event designed to promote development of an airport, the local chapter of the National Aeronautic Association argued, "Were we prepared we could have a Reserve unit of the United States Army Air Service," in the National Air Congress souvenir program.

Military aviation had a similar inauspicious beginning. The nation's first foray into military airpower occurred with balloons during the Civil War. Filled with hydrogen gas, "Professor" Thaddeus Lowe's observation balloons monitored Confederate troop positions along the battle lines. Less than 50 years later, the U.S. Army owned its first airplane. America's air arm was on its way. McConnell Air Force Base's initial development as a U.S. Air Force base began as Europe was embroiled in World War II. Just months before Pearl Harbor, the Air National Guard established the 127th Observation Squadron at Wichita Municipal Airport. Throughout the war years, operations consisted largely of military procurement at the local aircraft plants. With the war's end, the jet age dawned, and McConnell Air Force Base became a reality.

Here is America's first military aviation. The observation balloon *Intrepid* prepares to launch on the Virginia peninsula June 18, 1862. (Courtesy Library of Congress.)

Grand visions often begin modestly. Clyde Cessna, one of the great pioneers of Wichita's aviation industry, flies his first plane, the *Silverwing*, over the Oklahoma Salt Flats in 1912. Cessna would, 30 years later like other Wichita manufacturers, produce aircraft for the U.S. Army Air Corps and the U.S. Navy. (Courtesy Kansas Aviation Museum.)

Wichita was a hotbed of growth for the aviation industry from its earliest days, and its citizens enthusiastically took hold of the new technology. Here a group of student pilots stand in front of a brand new Swallow aircraft outside the Swallow Airplane Manufacturing Company. The size of the group speaks to the local interest in flying. (Courtesy Office of History, 22d Air Refueling Wing.)

The Swallow Airplane Manufacturing Company was no better represented than by its titular aircraft. Depicted here is a 1924 model of the "new" Swallow. (Courtesy Office of History, 22d Air Refueling Wing.)

Swallow Airplane Manufacturing Company did more than just build airplanes. As was typical of many companies from the early days of aviation, they also trained pilots and offered flights both for thrill seeking and actual trips. The factory's sign in this 1924 photograph advertises, "$2.50 Per Passenger For Flight Over City, $3.00 Per 2 Passengers For Flight Over City and 20¢ Per Mile For Any Distance Over 200 Miles." (Courtesy Office of History, 22d Air Refueling Wing.)

Jake Mollendick was arguably the man most responsible for launching Wichita's aviation industry. His temper and stubbornness are as legendary as his willingness to take risk. This photograph, taken on January 20, 1925, depicts Mollendick on the far left with three of his Swallow Airplane Manufacturing Company employees as they prepared the 1925 model Swallow behind them for an aviation event called The Detroit Tour. Mollendick eventually went broke promoting the growth of aviation and died penniless. (Courtesy Kansas Aviation Museum.)

Military aviation also began slowly. Early pilot training often employed crude devices. This advertisement from the June 14, 1920, issue of *Aerial Age Weekly*, depicts the Ruggles Orientator, a device utilized to familiarize and train early airmen on the phenomenon known as "spatial disorientation," which is a common occurrence in aircraft. Similar devices, such as the Barney Chair, are still utilized in this manner by the U.S. Air Force. (Courtesy Kansas Aviation Museum.)

By the mid-1920s, the California Section, future home of McConnell Air Force Base, was already regularly launching and landing aircraft. In 1929, the first permanent structure, an airport hangar, was constructed on the site. This mid-1930s photograph depicts several early Wichita aviation pioneers. Depicted here are, from left to right, Carl Winstead, Don George, Preston Kirk, Charles Lander, E. B. Christopher, Havel While, Ed Opperman, James Zimmerman, John Free, Deed Levy, N. L. Sifers, Frank Straughan, Ted Peaso, W. P. Huston, George Theis, Sam Robertson, and Joe Patterson. (Courtesy Kansas Aviation Museum.)

The first building finished and in use on McConnell Air Force Base was a sales and service hangar for the Stearman Aircraft Company. Opened in 1929, the hangar was the first in the nation to utilize cantilevered hangar doors. In the photograph above, a 1932 Stearman model 6H trainer rests in front of the hangar. The photograph below shows the hangar after it was struck by a tornado shortly after opening. The building still stands on McConnell Air Force Base today and is utilized by the Civil Air Patrol. (Courtesy Kansas Aviation Museum.)

Aviation was often promoted in what one might today perceive as odd ways. This staged photograph from 1928 for what appears to be a Richfield aviation gas promotion, pilot Charles Meyers sips on coffee brought to him by two waitresses while the Richfield mechanic fills Meyers's Waco Taper Wing aircraft, also adorned with a Richfield tail flash. This photograph may have been taken on the California Section, which while in use for flying at this time, did not feature any sort of dining facilities. The photograph is a bit whimsical. (Courtesy Kansas Aviation Museum.)

Early aviation was not all fun and games. Tragedies were both frequent and unpredictable with early aircraft. On March 31, 1931, legendary football coach Knute Rockne lost his life in this plane crash near the town of Bazzar. As seen in the photograph, then as now, a few morbid thrill seekers appear to take some delight in being recorded for posterity at the scene while others are decidedly more somber. (Courtesy Kansas Aviation Museum.)

Clarence D. Chamberlain's Curtiss Condor sits outside the airport's hangar sometime in the late 1930s or early 1940s. The Condor was an early commercial transportation aircraft with a very brief construction period that began in 1933 and ended in 1937. Though relatively few were produced, Condors were important to early transcontinental passenger travel. (Courtesy Kansas Aviation Museum.)

On the eve of World War II, Wichita Municipal Airport was a thriving Midwest stop over for transcontinental travel. The art deco–style terminal building is shown here in a photograph from the early 1940s.

The airport's conversion began on the eve of World War II. In the summer of 1941, the Kansas Air National Guard (KANG) activated at the airport. Wichita received its first permanent U.S. Air Force presence with this unit's activation. This photograph, taken shortly after unit activation, shows nearly everybody initially assigned to the local KANG. (Courtesy Office of Public Affairs, 184th Intelligence Wing.)

This is a U.S. Army Air Force photograph showing an aerial view of Wichita Municipal Airport. This image can be dated to around 1942, as it shows the completed National Guard armory building (square structure with courtyard at right) constructed in 1941, the airport's hangar which burned to the ground in 1945, and several medium bombers on the Boeing ramp at left. Also visible are the Planeview and Hilltop housing districts built for Boeing workers. (Courtesy Office of History, 22d Air Refueling Wing.)

A man known for both his cartooning and vast knowledge of Abraham Lincoln, Lloyd Ostendorf spent World War II as an enlisted man involved in military procurement. These two cartoons well illustrate his wry sense of humor. The comic above illustrates *The Caveman Bomber B-1* while the cartoon below, entitled *The Armament Nightmare*, lampoons the Manhattan Project. In both cases, one sees satire utilized to demonstrate engineer's problems with the sometimes demanding requirements of the U.S. Department of War. These cartoons circulated as Christmas cards through the research and development departments at Wright Field in Dayton. (Courtesy Office of History, 22d Air Refueling Wing.)

While war production and nascent military activity continued in Wichita and at the airport, regular commercial activity also went on in a relatively unabated manner as commercial air traffic through Wichita continued on the rise. This photograph from the 1940s shows airport employees preparing to place "air stairs" up to a just-landed Braniff Airways DC-3 commercial passenger plane. The gentleman in white coat and cap is a porter wheeling a baggage cart. (Courtesy Kansas Aviation Museum.)

Military aircraft development often provided breaks from the routine for local citizens. In this photograph, an Army Air Force Beechcraft UC-43 buzzes a group of local farmers in a wheat field near Wichita about 1942. The *UC* moniker indicates "Utility-Cargo," meaning the aircraft had a number of uses. Most commonly, UC-43s were utilized as light passenger transports to carry high-ranking officials and military officers. Its civilian variant was the Model 17 Stagger Wing. (Courtesy Kansas Aviation Museum.)

America's technological capabilities continued to grow through the war years, and the bombers constructed became more complex. As the war moved forward, Boeing began production of the B-29 heavy bomber. This photograph shows a number of B-29s under construction at the Boeing Wichita plant, now owned by Spirit Aero Systems. The U.S. Air Force officer in charge of B-29 procurement became a legend in August 1945. His name was Col. Paul W. Tibbetts. (Courtesy Air Force Historical Research Agency.)

Here is Colonel Tibbetts with the *Enola Gay* at Walker Air Force Base in Roswell, New Mexico, some time following the drop of the atomic bomb on Hiroshima. Colonel Tibbetts pulled two tours of duty in Wichita, first from 1943 to 1944 to oversee the B-29 project, and again from 1950 to 1952 to oversee procurement of the B-47 Stratojet. Legend holds that it was Tibbetts personal recommendation that clinched the establishment of an air force base in Wichita. (Courtesy U.S. Air Force.)

Regardless of the strong U.S. Air Force presence existing under Col. Paul W. Tibbetts, several state leaders including some congressmen were against establishing a base in Wichita. Kansas's senior U.S. senator Andrew Schoeppel (pictured here in a gubernatorial portrait) was lobbied heavily and initially came out against establishing Wichita Air Force Base. Over 40 air force bases had been built in Kansas during the war, and many saw no need to construct a new one. Schoeppel was won over in favor of the air base in pretty short order, and by summer of 1950, the decision was final. (Courtesy Kansas Aviation Museum.)

The U.S. Air Force announced on March 16, 1951, that the first commander of Wichita Air Force Base would be Col. Henry "H. R." Spicer. Colonel Spicer was a fighter pilot in World War II. Decorated with the Distinguished Flying Cross and also having spent time as a prisoner of war, Colonel Spicer was often as no-nonsense as his portrait here would indicate. Colonel Spicer's image here illustrates two fundamental changes in officers since earlier years. Open use of tobacco and wear of facial hair is nearly unheard of today. (Courtesy of Mark Schock.)

When Wichita Air Force Base opened for business on April 2, 1951, it was still an airport. Living quarters were necessary. The U.S. Air Force immediately began construction of a tent city to house junior enlisted personnel. Eventually 174 tents were built near Planeview on the northwest side of the base. (Courtesy Office of History, 22d Air Refueling Wing.)

Life in the tent city could be tough on the young GIs. These canvas tents were neither air conditioned in summer nor heated with fuel oil stoves in winter. As any Kansas resident knows, summer in the state is hot. The expressions of these two airmen pulling sentry duty at the tent city seem to express their feelings about life in the tents. (Courtesy Mark Schock.)

The winter of 1951 brought disaster to the men in the tents when a November snowstorm blanketed the area. Some of them though took it with a sense of humor. In the photograph above, Airman Second Class Richard Schock, left, and an unidentified airman stand outside for a photograph. The photograph below depicts Schock on the right with another unidentified airman. Following this snowfall, barracks construction took on a slightly more rapid pace. (Courtesy Mark Schock.)

Until the mid-1980s, regularly occurring drills were a part of routine life on an air force base. Retirement ceremonies for instance often received a "pass in review." This 1952 photograph illustrates a pass in review. (Courtesy Mark Schock.)

Enlisted airmen's lives significantly improved when their barracks were finished in 1952. Depicted here is Airmen First Class Robert Dellapenna, a B-47 crew chief. These barracks underwent a number of modifications over the years that significantly changed the interiors from the original open bays to private rooms. The bulk was destroyed by the Andover tornado in 1991. The last of them was demolished in 2008. (Courtesy of SMSgt. [retired] Robert Dellpenna).

The primary mission of Wichita Air Force Base was combat crew training for the pilots and navigators that flew the B-47. Few sites were more impressive, or loud for that matter, than a B-47 performing a rocket assisted take-off (RATO). Such RATO flights were performed with the use of nine rockets on either side of the planes fuselage that added additional thrust just as shown in this 1952 launch. (Courtesy Mark Schock.)

Life was not always drudgery in the air base's early days. In this photograph from 1952, Airman Second Class Richard Schock (foreground right) along with two fellow airmen and some lady friends spend an evening drinking and dancing at the Trig Ballroom on East Kellogg Avenue in Wichita. (Courtesy Mark Schock.)

Just as Schock and his companions enjoyed the city, so did Airman Second Class Robert Dellapenna, shown here taking a stroll down Douglass Avenue in downtown Wichita on a sunny 1953 day. (Courtesy SMSgt. [retired] Robert Dellapenna.)

Promotion is a proud moment for any airman, officer or enlisted. Here 2nd Lt. Harry Middlebrook (left) of the 3520th Headquarters Squadron and John Klepinger (right) of the Exchange are promoted to 1st Lt. by Col. Leslie Holman, commander of the 3520th Combat Support Group. (Courtesy Office of History, McConnell Air Force Base.)

As the base continued flying training for the U.S. Air Force, Boeing Wichita continued turning out B-47s. A momentous occurrence conveniently occurred on December 17, 1954, when Boeing delivered the 1,000th B-47 to the U.S. Air Force. Pictured here at left is Dean Cunningham and at far right Bob Perry, both Boeing test pilots. The others are unidentified. (Courtesy Kansas Aviation Museum.)

A part of life on every military base are regularly scheduled open houses. These events allow the public to view up close the military mission. McConnell Air Force Base has been no different over the years. This 1952 photograph shows visitors examining an array of audio-visual equipment from the communications squadron while a staff sergeant answers questions in the background. (Courtesy Mark Schock.)

This is another photograph from the 1952 open house. An unidentified adult helps children climb into and out of a U.S. Army tank. Open houses just as frequently feature exhibits and equipment of their sister services just as they do their own. (Courtesy Mark Schock.)

The B-47 with its swept wings and multiple jets engines was a bomber like no other before it. This often led to dramatic moments in the plane's early life, particularly at a training base like Wichita. This 1952 photograph shows a B-47 making a gear up belly landing on the runway. (Courtesy Kansas Aviation Museum.)

A frequently asked question concerns the name of the air base. McConnell Air Force Base originally opened as Wichita Air Force Base, but in April 1954, the U.S. Air Force renamed it for the "Flying McConnells" from Wichita. Pictured here in the their flight gear about 1943 are, from left to right, Thomas, Fred, and Edwin McConnell. (Courtesy Office of History, 22d Air Refueling Wing.)

Dedication of McConnell Air Force Base took place on May 15, 1954, to mark Armed Forces Day. Many dignitaries turned out for the event. This photograph shows a handful of them. From left to right are, Col. Louis Coira, McConnell's commander; Brig. Gen. Henry R. Spicer, vice commander U.S. Air Force crew training; Rep. Howard Schultz (D-KS); Sen. Herbert Rees (R-KS); Maj. Gen. Glenn Barcus, vice commander of Air Training Command; and Sen. Frank Carlson (R-KS). (Courtesy Office of History, 22d Air Refueling Wing.)

Mary Lou McConnell, the widow of Fred McConnell, and two of their children, Tommy and Kittie Lou, pose with the dedication plaque honoring their father and his brother Thomas at the May 15, 1954, base dedication. (Courtesy Office of History, 22d Air Refueling Wing.)

Kittie Lou cuts the cake at the Officer's Club following the ceremony while her brother Tommy looks on. Kittie Lou was named the guest of honor for the dedication ceremony. (Courtesy Office of History, 22d Air Refueling Wing.)

Here is a very rare photograph of the three McConnell brothers during flight training at Luke Field (now Luke Air Force Base) in Arizona. At far left is Thomas, third from left is Fred, and at far right is Edwin. They and their friends are partaking in a breakfast of pancakes on a rare day off. (Courtesy Office of History, 22d Air Refueling Wing.)

The brothers gained a lot of regional notoriety when they joined, trained, and served in the same unit together. Local papers followed them to include staging a photo-op of a proud moment for their mother. Anna McConnell pins pilot's wings on Thomas McConnell while Fred and Edwin (left to right, respectively) look on. Their cap badges still show their status as aviation cadets. (Courtesy Office of History, 22d Air Refueling Wing.)

DECEMBER . . . CALENDAR OF ACTIVITIES

SUN.	MON.	TUE.	WED.	THU.	FRI.	SAT.
	1	2 N.C.O. Wives Club Meeting 7:30	3 Bingo Two Jack-Pots Each Week	4	5	6 Monta Carlo Night 2000 – 0100
7 Air-Lane Trio 6 Till 9	8	9	10 Bingo	11	12	13 "Capitol-Airs" Base Band 2100-0100
14 Air-Lane Trio 6 Till 9	15	16	17 Bingo 12 Turkeys and Prizes Jack-Pot	18	19 5c Beer and Dutch Lunch	20 ? 2100-0100
21 Air-Lane Trio 6 Till 9	22	23	24 Xmas Eve.	25 Xmas Day	26	27 "Capitol-Airs" Base Band 2100-0100
28 Air-Lane Trio 6 Till 9	29	30	31 New Year's Eve Dance 9 - ? Howie Phillips	1 New Year's Day – Sober-Up		

This document indicates U.S. Air Force–sponsored "morale and welfare" activities of the early 1950s. This monthly club card for December 1952 lays out the events available at the NCO (noncommissioned officer) open mess. A sure sign of a different era must be the scheduled activity for New Year's Day: "Sober Up." (Courtesy Office of History, 22d Air Refueling Wing.)

Many outcomes resulted in tragedy. A sad but recurring practice in the base's early days was to conduct memorial dedications of base structures in honor of those who lost their lives in training accidents. This 1959 photograph is from the dedication ceremony for Edwards Hall. Memorialization still occurs on McConnell Air Force Base to this day. Spicer Court in base housing is named in honor of the base's first commander, Col. Henry "H. R." Spicer. (Courtesy Office of History, 22d Air Refueling Wing.)

Capt. Herbert Edwards perished in a B-47 crash on November 17, 1959. He left behind his wife and young daughter as survivors. Captain Edwards received five Air Medals in World War II among other decorations. (Courtesy Office of History, 22d Air Refueling Wing.)

The B-47 was a versatile jet. The aircraft was also capable of other missions depending on its model configuration. The B-47K for instance conducted photograph reconnaissance. Pictured here with a wide array of the gear utilized on a B-47K are, from left to right, Bob Perry, unidentified, and Rod Randall. (Courtesy Kansas Aviation Museum.)

Spiritual considerations have long been important to the armed forces, and McConnell Air Force Base was no exception. One of the first buildings to mark completion was the base chapel which opened in the summer of 1952. The chief of the U.S. Air Force chaplain's service conducted the formal dedication and local radio station KFH covered the service. This photograph was taken shortly after that event. (Courtesy Mark Schock.)

A group of Cub Scouts check out the engine intake of a North American F-86 Sabre Jet during an air show in the 1950s. The Kansas Air National Guard's 184th Fighter Group flew Sabre Jets from 1958 until 1961, when they were replaced by Lockheed's F-80 Shooting Star. (Courtesy Office of History, 22d Air Refueling Wing.)

Two

MISSILES, FIGHTERS, AND COLD WAR 1962–1986

As the 1950s drew to a close, tensions between the United States and the Soviet Union began to reach a fevered pitch. The B-47 era was a result of these tensions. Events took a more dramatic turn though as nuclear arms proliferation moved from the skies to space itself. The Soviets had launched the Sputnik satellite, and both sides had been experimenting with missile and rocket technology almost as soon as the ink was dry on the surrender documents of World War II in 1945.

For its part, the United States had by the late 1950s and early 1960s begun the development of intercontinental ballistic missiles, or ICBMs. These missiles were propelled by rocket power into low earth orbit where they would then release their reentry vehicle which contained a nuclear warhead. One of the first major ICBMs was the Titan I. This was rapidly followed with the Titan II missile. This latter missile played an important role at McConnell Air Force Base. Beginning in 1962, the U.S. Air Force ended McConnell Air Force Base's B-47 program in favor of using the base to support a strategic missile wing. Silo construction began and moved with lightening fast pace. A total of 18 missile silos encircled the greater Wichita area for the next 20 years. The threat of global thermonuclear war would be a daily reminder for the men and now women assigned to McConnell Air Force Base and the surrounding communities.

Occurring simultaneously to this was another event that would shape the entirety of the 1960s and ultimately create fundamental changes in how the United States would employ their armed forces in the future. Increasing involvement and escalation of American military activity in Vietnam also affected McConnell Air Force Base. Through the 1960s, no less than three different fighter wings took up residence at the base alongside the missileers. All of them with one purpose in mind: ultimate deployment to Southeast Asia and the Vietnam War.

Here is the end of an era. This staged publicity photograph from 1960 shows a B-47 crew in a "Race For Security." The big tip offs as to its being staged are that side arms were left aboard alert jets, not carried, and the position of their alert car. (Courtesy Kansas Aviation Museum.)

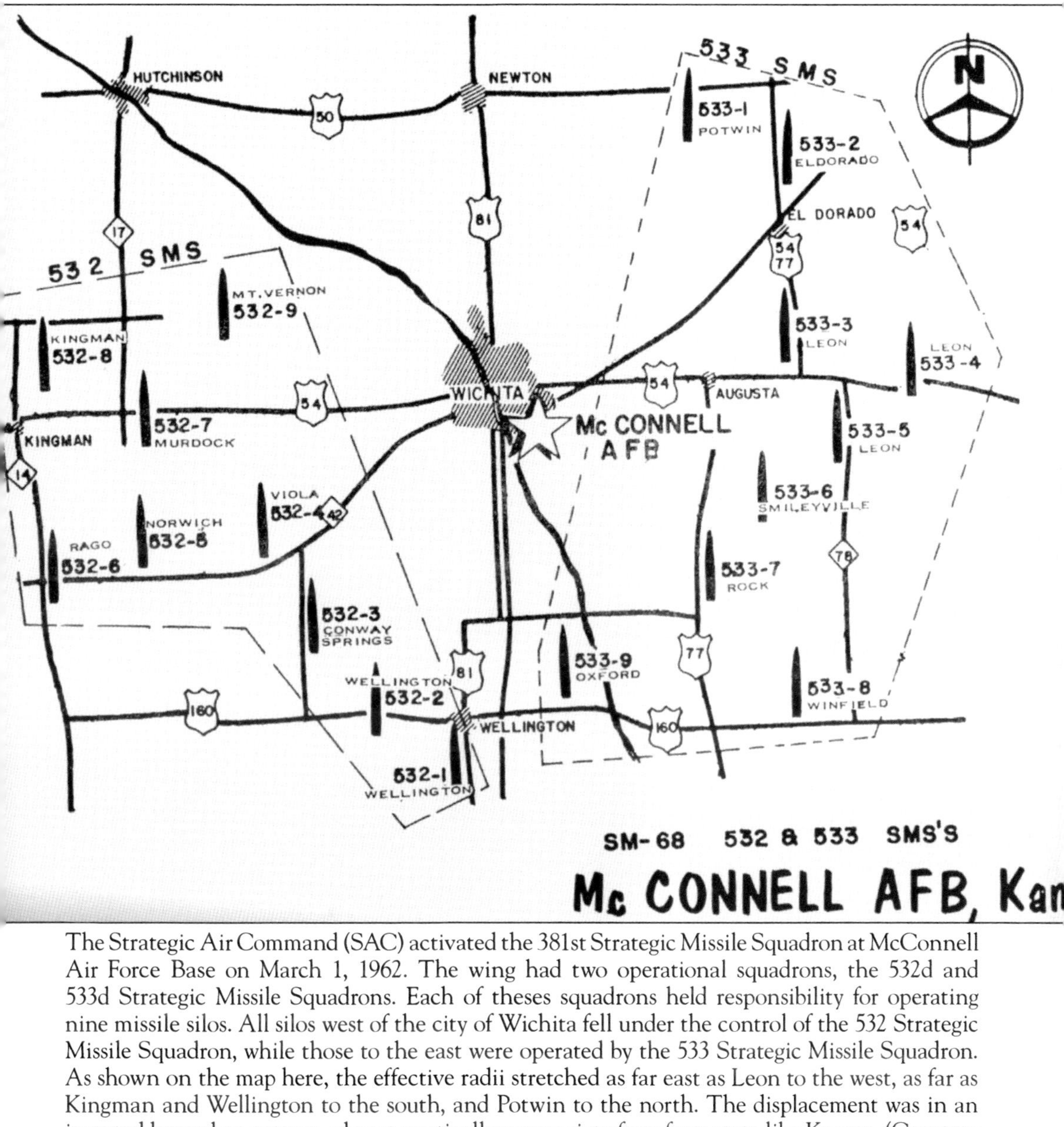

The Strategic Air Command (SAC) activated the 381st Strategic Missile Squadron at McConnell Air Force Base on March 1, 1962. The wing had two operational squadrons, the 532d and 533d Strategic Missile Squadrons. Each of theses squadrons held responsibility for operating nine missile silos. All silos west of the city of Wichita fell under the control of the 532 Strategic Missile Squadron, while those to the east were operated by the 533 Strategic Missile Squadron. As shown on the map here, the effective radii stretched as far east as Leon to the west, as far as Kingman and Wellington to the south, and Potwin to the north. The displacement was in an inverted horseshoe pattern, almost poetically appropriate for a farm state like Kansas. (Courtesy Office of History, 22d Air Refueling Wing.)

Missile launch complexes or silos were outwardly simple affairs and very easy to miss from the ground. This aerial photograph of complex 532-4 near Viola illustrates the point. Aside from the blast doors in the center of the complex, little appears to indicate what this facility would be used for. Surrounded by farmland, most views of these silos would be obscured from public view by the crops growing around them. (Courtesy Office of History, 22d Air Refueling Wing.)

Col. George Van Arb was the first of the 381st Strategic Missile Wing (SMW) commanders at McConnell Air Force Base. During World War II, the 381st was a bombardment unit. (Courtesy Office of History, 22d Air Refueling Wing.)

Depicted here is a test launch of a Titan II missile at Vandenburg Air Force Base. None of McConnell Air Force Base's Titans were ever fired, since all were on constant alert for offensive use. Selected missile wing launch crews would on occasion travel to Vandenburg Air Force Base to execute experimental launches such as this one. (Courtesy Office of History, 22d Air Refueling Wing.)

Given the distances between McConnell Air Force Base and its silos varied from roughly 20 to 50 miles, rapid transport to and from the complexes was always an issue. One for the methods used was light aircraft. In this photograph from April 1963, a DeHavilland U-6A Beaver lands at complex 532-1 with Capt. John L. Terpening as pilot. The 381 SMW utilized this method for a while before switching to UH series helicopters. (Courtesy Office of History, 22d Air Refueling Wing.)

Within two years of SAC activating the 381 SMW, the Tactical Air Command began a fighter wing operation at the air base as the B-47 operations phased out. Col. Richard E. Vanbury, pictured here, became the first local commander of the 388th Tactical Fighter Wing (TFW). The wing remained at McConnell Air Force Base for only 15 months. (Courtesy Office of History, 22d Air Refueling Wing.)

On February 8, 1964, one of the legendary units in U.S. Air Force history arrived at McConnell Air Force Base. The Flying Tigers of the 23 TFW made their name in World War II. In the photograph, Airman First Class David L. Rogers presents the wing colors to Lt. Gen. Bruce K. Holloway (left), commander of U.S. Strike Command, and new wing commander Col. Jack R. Best. (Courtesy Office of History, 22d Air Refueling Wing.)

A focus on family is a decades old hallmark of the U.S. Air Force. What are now called Airmen and Family Readiness Centers initially began as Family Support Centers. This 1966 photograph illustrates a small portion of service they provided as a young enlisted person signs out loaner dishes for his family to use. (Courtesy Office of History, 22d Air Refueling Wing.)

Though F-100s were flown at McConnell Air Force Base, they only did so briefly. The most common jet fighter in the Wichita skies through the 1960s was the F-105 Thunderchief or "Thud." This June 7, 1969, photograph depicts an F-105F of the 561st Tactical Fighter Squadron (TFS) sitting on the McConnell ramp. Tail flashes are the easiest way to identify an aircraft's squadron. The *MD* on this jet places it in the 561 TFS. (Courtesy Kansas Aviation Museum.)

Formation flying is always a site to behold. In early 1964, 16 Thuds from the 563 TFS took to the Wichita skies and did a flyover of the base in formation. This photograph shows the squadron formed up together. (Courtesy Office of History, 22d Air Refueling Wing.)

While women began joining the U.S. Air Force as early as 1948, it was not until the 1970s that one noticed more and more female airmen. Two McConnell Air Force Base women made American and U.S. Air Force history in 1978. Airman First Class Tina Ponzer (right) and 1st Lt. Patricia Fornes (below) became the first women to serve on an alert missile launch crew. Ponzer went first when she pulled her initial tour in August 1978. Fornes took her first alert tour in September. (Courtesy Office of History, 22d Air Refueling Wing.)

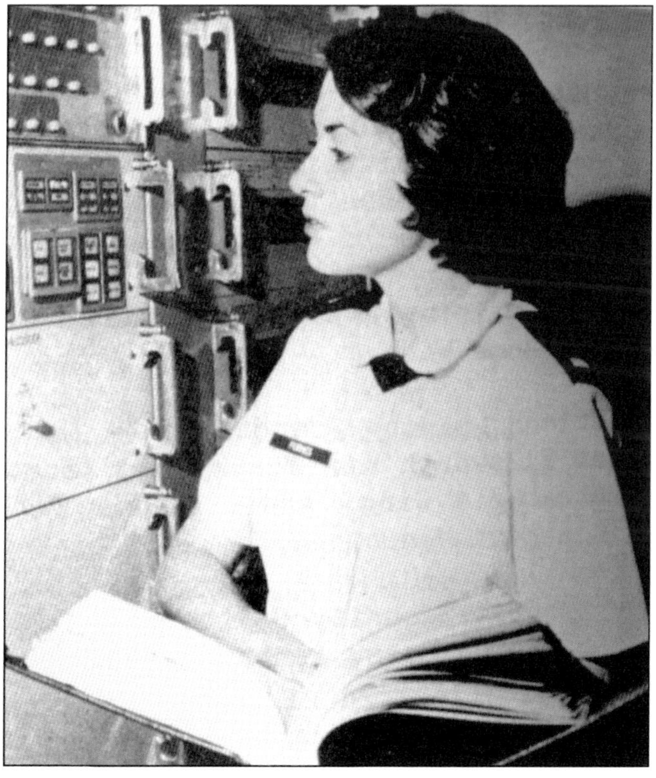

Sometimes there were moments of glory, sometimes moments of drudgery. Detail work is as old as military service itself. This 1977 photograph depicts Airman First Class Brenda Stephens of the 381st Missile Maintenance Squadron preparing for a Commander's Annual Facility Inspection (CAFI) by painting a door jamb. Legends of SAC airmen painting the dirt green and rocks gray are not far from the truth as this photograph indicates. (Courtesy Office of History 22d Air Refueling Wing.)

Titan II maintenance work was dangerous, particularly when handling the nitrogen tetroxide fuel used as propellant. On August 24, 1978, an improperly seated quick release valve did not seal, and 13,000 gallons of the corrosive fuel leaked out into silo 533-7 near Rock. SSgt. Robert J. Thomas and Airman First Class Erby Hepstall both perished in this accident. The dark cloud is a sulfur gas produced when the silo was flooded with water to neutralize the rocket fuel. (Courtesy Office of History, 22d Air Refueling Wing.)

Major accidents such as the fuel leak launch major investigations. A safety investigation board, or SIB, immediately looks to determine causation. This 1978 photograph illustrates just how dangerous the accident was. SIB members prepare to enter silo 533-7 by donning rocket fuel handler's coverall outfits, or RFHCOs. Resembling space suits, RFHCOs protected persons exposed to the caustic nitrogen tetroxide via self-containment. (Courtesy Office of History, 22d Air Refueling Wing.)

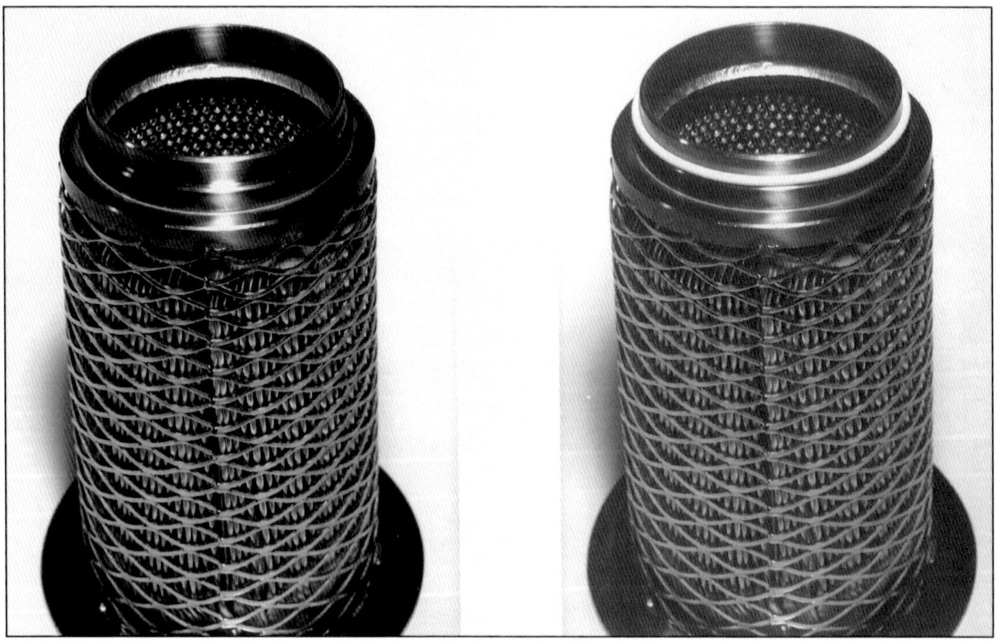

This split photograph illustrates what went wrong in silo 533-7. The photograph on the left shows the filter of the quick disconnect coupling as it was in the silo. The one on the right shows the filter as it should appear with a white "O" ring that acted as a seal. A simple missing ring led to a tragic disaster. (Courtesy Office of History, 22d Air Refueling Wing.)

The 381 SMW also experienced numerous successes during their time at McConnell Air Force Base. The wing was one of the best ICBM forces in the U.S. Air Force as clearly illustrated here when the "McConnell Machine" won the Blanchard Trophy in 1977 as the absolute best missile wing in the U.S. Air Force. (Courtesy Office of History, 22d Air Refueling Wing.)

Another first for McConnell Air Force Base was Col. Elmer T. Brooks (later a brigadier general). When he took command of the 381 SMW on January 19, 1979, Brooks became the first, and to date only, African American to lead an operational wing at McConnell Air Force Base. (Courtesy Office of History, 22d Air Refueling Wing.)

The 184th Tactical Fighter Group (TFG) of the Kansas Air National Guard produced a first of their own. This group of airmen represent the first women to serve in the unit. At far right in the front row is Cheryl Fellows, the very first female member of the 184 TFG when she joined on April 6, 1970. This photograph dates from about 1975. (Courtesy Office of Public Affairs, 184th Intelligence Wing).

Military units enjoy their fun too. That fun produced another first for the 184 TFG. These gentlemen finished first and second in the bathtub races at the 1978 Wichita River Festival. The annual week-long street party has long been enjoyed not just by the citizens of Wichita but also their military neighbors. (Courtesy Office of Public Affairs, 184th Intelligence Wing.)

In April 1971, the U.S. Air Force began a strategic air refueling operation at McConnell Air Force Base in support of the ongoing nuclear alert posture that the U.S. Air Force maintained. Beginning with the 91st Air Refueling Squadron and later the 384th Air Refueling Squadron, SAC began 24-7 alert duty. That did not seem to bother this group of KC-135 mechanics, proudly posing with a jet bearing a nod to Wichita as "Center City USA." (Courtesy Office of History, 22d Air Refueling Wing.)

Maintenance work is often backbreaking and takes place under nature's extremes. It can also produce moments of complete boredom when waiting on a jet as seen here. This group of aircraft maintainers sit inside their "bread truck" waiting for the jet to land in order to recover it. (Courtesy Office of History, 22d Air Refueling Wing.)

With the arrival of tanker aircraft, alert facility activities resumed for the first time since the B-47 era. This photograph depicts the alert facility as it looked in the mid- to late 1970s. Aircrews were literally locked down to the base for a week at a time and lived in this facility in case the Klaxon sounded, sending them to their jets and nuclear war. (Courtesy Office of History, McConnell Air Force Base.)

Life in the alert facility has some measures available to alleviate the boredom that often accompanied alert tours. Here a young officer, at left, watches as a boom operator prepares to take her shot in a photograph from the late 1970s. (Courtesy Office of History, 22d Air Refueling Wing.)

This is an aerial shot of McConnell Air Force Base taken in the late 1970s, most likely from a helicopter. Compared with earlier aerial views, the old California Section had turned into a sprawling layout. The old guard armory constructed in 1941 can be seen at the upper left, just in front of the flight line area. (Courtesy Kansas Aviation Museum.)

This aerial image of the Wichita Municipal Airport from the late 1940s provides excellent comparison to the image above taken 30 years later. Even though the airport was the second busiest in the nation at the time this photograph was taken, it appears to still be a sleepy place relative to the U.S. Air Force base of the 1970s depicted above. Nothing but farmland and trees existed on what is now a plot of land covered with all manner of buildings (Courtesy Kansas Aviation Museum.)

An old friend remains a silent witness to activity on the air base. With commercial work long since departed from McConnell Air Force Base, the old 1929 Stearman hangar still stood. By the 1970s it served as a hangar for McConnell Air Force Base's Aero Club. Aero clubs, though fewer in number now, exist to allow airmen with private pilot licenses to fly sport aircraft for morale and recreational purposes. McConnell Air Force Base's club operated until the mid-1980s, when falling membership and rising costs necessitated its closure. (Courtesy Office of History, 22d Air Refueling Wing.)

Another feature of McConnell Air Force Base during the missile years was the presence of UH series helicopters. Both the UH-1N such as the one pictured above and UH-1F birds were stationed at the base. These "Huey" choppers were used for flying emergency medical missions to the missile silos and rapid, unimpeded transport to the same. The photograph below shows a group of aeromedical technicians rushing back to their chopper following the August 1978 Rock silo accident. (Courtesy Office of History, 22d Air Refueling Wing.)

Friendly competitions among like units around the Air Force provide two things to the competitors. First of course is bragging rights. Second and more important, however, they validate training. The 384th Air Refueling Wing (ARW) excelled through the 1970s until its redesignation as a bombardment wing in 1988. Here members of the wing celebrate their win of the Saunders Trophy in 1980. (Courtesy Office of History, 22d Air Refueling Wing.)

The Saunders Trophy, depicted here after the 384 ARW's win in 1980, was presented to the best air refueling wing in SAC until the command was disbanded in 1994 under a U.S. Air Force–wide reorganization. Nearly all air refueling assets transferred to the new Air Mobility Command. (Courtesy Office of History, 22d Air Refueling Wing.)

Military units utilize exercises as methods of practicing and improving upon a variety of skills from combat related activity to natural disasters and accident response. Here some airmen assemble an immersion heater during a field exercise conducted on April 5 and 6, 1984. Early versions of meals-ready-to-eat (MREs) required use of a submersion heater since they did not yet have a self-contained heating element as today's MREs do. (Courtesy Office of History, 22d Air Refueling Wing.)

Occasionally exercises invoked interest of the local civilian press. A major accident response exercise that occurred in June of 1983 drew such interest. In this photograph, KSNW news reporter Kim Sherwood (back to camera) interviews SSgt. Mark K. Hess from the 381 SMW Public Affairs Office about the activity occurring behind Sergeant Hess. The local media have long held base activity newsworthy, and a long-standing professional bond has grown between them and various public affairs staffs of McConnell Air Force Base's many different wings. (Courtesy Office of History, 22d Air Refueling Wing.)

On occasion, joint exercises were and are conducted with the local community. This was particularly true of civil response organizations such as the base. A mass casualty exercise on May 18, 1984, involved McConnell Air Force Base's helicopter detachment with flying medics transporting patients to the helipad on top of St. Francis Hospital, as seen here. During the Titan II years, aeromedical technicians regularly flew both rescue and silo emergency flights. (Courtesy Office of History, 22d Air Refueling Wing.)

Exercises and competitions took place among the missile crews as well. This exercise from 1977, entitled Olympic Arena, evaluated both missile maintenance crews and launch crews. This photograph shows a 381 SMW launch crew at their stations in the silo complex's launch control facility. Two enlisted launch control technicians and two launch control officers comprised a launch crew. The senior officer served as the crew commander. (Courtesy Office of History, 22d Air Refueling Wing.)

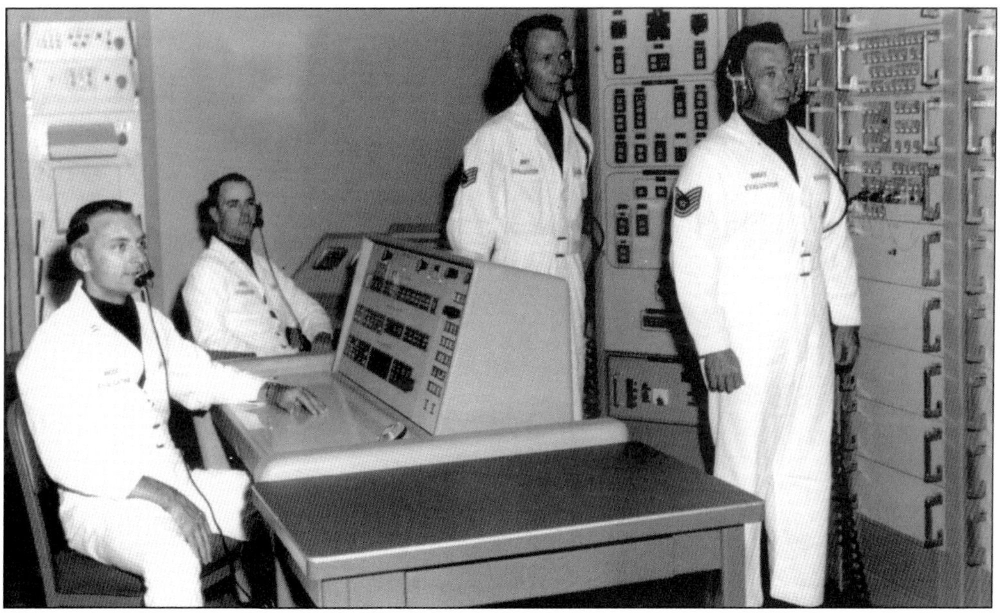

Every evaluation of a launch crew required an evaluator. This photograph from the 1970s shows one such evaluation team monitoring every move of a launch crew. No regular U.S. Air Force person thought of standardization and evaluation teams as being the good guy dressed in white. (Courtesy Office of History, 22d Air Refueling Wing.)

The last man to command an active duty fighter wing at McConnell Air Force Base was Col. Garry A. Willard Jr., depicted here. Colonel Willard commanded the 23 TFW from October 1, 1971, until its local inactivation on April 27, 1972. The Flying Tigers remain to this day, though now downsized to an active U.S. Air Force group based at Pope Air Force Base in North Carolina. (Courtesy Office of History, 22d Air Refueling Wing.)

This was a once-familiar site that is no more. A McDonnell F-4 Phantom II in flight over McConnell Air Force Base and the surrounding area was once common. Images such as this 1970s flight will not be seen again as the Thud is now retired, and fighter aircraft are no longer assigned. Directly above the aircraft, some of the 1952–1953 era barracks are visible. The last of these was razed in 2008. (Courtesy Office of History, 22d Air Refueling Wing.)

This view of Boeing on the west side of the flight line shows a large number of aircraft on the ramp, primarily B-52s and B-47s, which likely dates it to the 1960s since production of both appear to be in full swing. Longtime residents often insist that B-52s were assigned to McConnell Air Force Base, but this simply was never the case. The "Buffs" they saw were those being built or undergoing modification at Boeing. (Courtesy Office of History, 22d Air Refueling Wing.)

The F-105 was in many respects a great fighter aircraft. Along with the F-4, which by 1979 the 184 TFG switched to, the Thud was a workhorse in Vietnam. Many such as the one in this photograph from August 6, 1968, earned the devotion of their pilots and mechanics, as is evident here, as one clearly sees the crew chief wiping down the left wing pylon. (Courtesy Kansas Aviation Museum.)

As always, when one thing or another fades away on an U.S. Air Force base as an evolutionary step, some things never change such as official visits and open houses. The photograph above from August 23, 1983, marked a higher headquarters visit. From left to right, identified only as Sergeant Miller, dorm chief; Chief Lampe, the 381 SMW senior enlisted advisor; and the visitor, Chief Judd from the 19th Air Division, the three seem particularly interested in something off camera in this barracks room. In the photograph below, SSgt. Richard Schuster and his military working dog, Basil, put on a demonstration for the audience at the 1984 McConnell Air Show. (Courtesy Office of History, 22d Air Refueling Wing.)

As always during the Cold War, alert duty goes on. In this photograph, Capt. Mark Gale of the 384th Air Refueling Squadron checks a status board in the alert facility. Cold War alert duty was a way of life for a good portion of McConnell Air Force Base history. Nobody knew it then, but those days would come to a close soon. (Courtesy Office of History, 22d Air Refueling Wing.)

Another era in McConnell Air Force Base's history comes to an end. The first of McConnell Air Force Base's Titan II silos was deactivated on July 2, 1984, when silo 533-08 located outside of Winfield shut down, and as depicted in this 1984 photograph, the missile "downloaded." It took a crew of several maintainers to dismantle and remove the 103-foot-long missiles. (Courtesy Office of History, 22d Air Refueling Wing.)

Three

McConnell in Transition 1986–1994

With Pres. Ronald Reagan's announcement in 1984 that the Titan II ICBM program would end, host wing status transferred to the 384 ARW, which previously was a tenant organization on McConnell Air Force Base. The 381 SMW went about the business of slowly dismantling their missiles and rendering their silos that had stood for over 20 years on alert against the Soviet Union, inert. Some were exploded and filled, some ended up in private hands, even as residences. By November 1985, the last of the 381 SMW's work at McConnell was done and the unit inactivated.

The 384 ARW was also about to undergo a change. Originally a bombardment group in World War II, when it activated as a wing at McConnell Air Force Base in 1971, the organization was flying the KC-135A Stratotanker. All that changed in 1986. Reagan made the decision to revive the B-1 bomber program that his predecessor Pres. Jimmy Carter dropped from procurement after just two A model prototypes were built. The B-1 program was plagued through out the mid- to late 1970s with technological problems and cost overruns. Reagan saw the aircraft differently. By the mid-1980s, the aircraft were ready for operational assignment and McConnell Air Force Base would be home to a one-squadron bomb wing.

The 91st Air Refueling Squadron inactivated and the 384th Air Refueling Squadron was reassigned to the 19th Air Refueling Wing at Robins Air Force Base, Georgia, but operated at McConnell Air Force Base with 15 Stratotankers as a detached tenant unit. The era of the B-1 was underway. Part of the reasoning for splitting the tanker wing in half simply dealt with the lack of ramp space on the flight line. There was no chance of supporting 45 heavy aircraft, so this fact led to the removal of 15 tankers.

The fact was, though, this period of the B-1B Lancer was in actuality a period of transition. The bomb wing was based at McConnell only eight years. Growing pains for a new aircraft and the now waning Cold War led military leaders to view consolidation as the answer, and the B-1 disappeared from McConnell's active force almost as quickly as it came.

Base personnel move a Titan II reentry vehicle into the airpark as a museum piece in 1986. Behind it sits another relic of McConnell Air Force Base's past: an F-105. An era was over. (Courtesy Office of History, 22d Air Refueling Wing.)

Elected in 1976, Pres. Jimmy Carter was not a big fan of the B-1 procurement program. Cost estimates and program budget overruns were still an ongoing problem, and Carter, for his part, saw the development of cruise missiles as a wiser choice particularly with their versatile land, sea, and air launch capability. Carter cancelled the B-1 in 1977. (Courtesy Library of Congress.)

Just 10 months into office, Pres. Ronald Reagan reinstated the B-1B program almost as quickly as Carter had cancelled it. Reagan was convinced that a massive military build up that outpaced the Soviet Union's capability to match it was the quickest way to cooperation from the communist nation and end what had been a nearly 40-year quid pro quo. (Courtesy Library of Congress.)

While bomber activity pressed on, so did tanker modification. Beginning in 1983, the U.S. Air Force chose to re-engine the KC-135 fleet with more powerful, fuel-efficient engines. The first re-engined R model tanker was formally transferred to the 384th Air Refueling Squadron in 1986. The aircraft seen here is still in the McConnell Air Force Base fleet. (Courtesy Office of History, 22d Air Refueling Wing.)

To mark the occasion, the plane received special nose art to show a community connection to the city of Wichita. Wichita State University's mascot Wu Shock adorned the aircraft which also bore the sobriquet "Th' 'Shocker.'" (Courtesy Office of History, 22d Air Refueling Wing.)

The conversion to R model utilizing the CFM-54 engines resulted in major changes in the performance of the KC-135. This photograph from the mid-1980s gives one an appreciation for the size of the engine intakes as a young boy of about six or seven sits more than comfortably inside. (Courtesy Office of History, 22d Air Refueling Wing.)

The U.S. Air Force wished to validate their new R model tankers both for the American public and to the always-watching Soviets. On November 19, 1988, the *Cherokee Rose* set 16 different world records, some set by a crew from the 384th Air Refueling Squadron. Maj. Rod Bell, Capt. Jim Melancon, Capt. Julie Keck, and MSgt. Stan Sears set the first record of the day besting the record of the even lighter Soviet YAK-42. (Courtesy 22d Air Refueling Wing Public Affairs.)

The 384 ARW was officially redesignated in a ceremony on July 1987. Here wing commander Col. Phillip J. Ford (center) furls and cases the wing flag of the 384 ARW moments before unfurling a new one labeled 384th Bombardment Wing. (Courtesy Office of History, 22d Air Refueling Wing.)

When all systems were go, the early editions of the B-1B illustrated how devastating their offensive capability could be. This photograph depicts a 384th Bombardment Wing (BMW) practice run at the Smoky Hills range near Salina. This "bone" is dropping a large amount of ordinance while also releasing flares as a defensive counter measure. Smoky Hills is operated by a National Guard detachment of the 184th based at McConnell Air Force Base. (Courtesy Office of History, 22d Air Refueling Wing.)

The B-1s of the 384 BMW never dropped a bomb in combat. This photograph, from a March 10, 2008, air strike in Zambraniyah, Iraq, on an insurgent torture house gives one an idea of the deadly nature of the Lancer's power. The strike utilized six guided bomb units, or GBUs. (Courtesy Department of Defense.)

Another SAC competition garnered another Saunders Trophy. Col. Charles "Tony" Robertson (light shirt on left), 384 BMW commander, celebrates with his crews at the 1989 SAC Bomb-Nav competition. Regardless of designation, the unit continued to win U.S. Air Force–level awards. (Courtesy Office of History, 22d Air Refueling Wing.)

Col. Charles Robertson had one of the more illustrious careers of McConnell Air Force Base's many wing commanders. A 1968 graduate of the U.S. Air Force Academy, Robertson was a command pilot with flying time in over 20 aircraft and was twice awarded the Distinguished Flying Cross. He retired as a four-star general and commander of Air Mobility Command in 2001. (Courtesy Office of History, 22d Air Refueling Wing.)

Just how dangerous is aerial refueling? This photograph perhaps gives one a perception of the precarious nature of the task. Taken out of the boom operator's window at the rear of the aircraft, it is obvious AC-130 gunships get very large when up close and personal as this one is while hooking to a McConnell Air Force Base tanker over the Adriatic Sea. (Courtesy Office of History, 22d Air Refueling Wing.)

While the flying of bombers and tankers continued unabated through the 1980s and early 1990s, so did the seemingly more mundane tasks associated with the operation of a major U.S. Air Force wing. Exercises continued, as illustrated in the photograph above of a 384th Security Police Squadron staff sergeant guarding the door to the command post and the photograph below featuring SSgt. Randall Brown, an enlisted historian assigned to document the wing's activities for posterity. While the active U.S. Air Force moved to hiring degreed civilians for the history program, the enlisted paraprofessionals continue to ply their trade with dedication in the Air Force Reserve. (Courtesy Office of History, 22d Air Refueling Wing.)

Disaster struck McConnell Air Force Base on April 26, 1991, at about 6:30 p.m. A major tornado that eventually grew to an F-5 strength struck the base and continued northeast into the city of Andover nearly flattening the entire town. This photograph was taken by a decidedly brave airman standing on the fire escape of one of the barracks buildings as the funnel was just entering the air base from the southwest. (Courtesy Office of History, 22d Air Refueling Wing.)

Here the tornado slams into the Delta P Snack Bar and Foster Lanes bowling alley. It would continue on through the base going straight through the front doors of the hospital, across Rock Road to the east, and into base housing. Despite its size and incredible damage, only 16 injuries occurred, all of them minor. (Courtesy Office of History, 22d Air Refueling Wing.)

These are the remains of the Delta P Snack Bar and Foster Lanes bowling alley. A popular stop for lunch or after-work recreation, these facilities, along with the equally destroyed NCO club, were acutely missed by the base population. The Officer's Club became a temporary consolidated mess until the opening of a new consolidated community center called Emerald City in 1994. (Courtesy Office of History, 22d Air Refueling Wing.)

Foster Lanes lasted for 30 years. The building was dedicated to a B-47 crew member, Capt. Byron C. Foster, who lost his life in a Stratojet crash. The photograph here was taken at the time of the official dedication of the building. The woman at the center of the photograph is presumably the widow of the aforementioned Foster.

This is the original billeting office prior to the tornado. The structure was one of the original buildings constructed in the 1952–1953 period. Damage as a result of the tornado necessitated construction of a new lodging facility, the Air Capital Inn, which is now one of the premiere billeting operations in the U.S. Air Force. (Courtesy Office of History, 22d Air Refueling Wing.)

This aerial view of the base hospital was taken on April 27, 1991, the day after the tornado struck the base. A total of 102 housing units and 9 major facilities were destroyed by the twister. Inside the hospital, medical staff moved the small number of inpatients into an enclosed interior hallway, likely preventing further injury to McConnell Air Force Base personnel. The storm hit outpatient areas, which were already closed for the evening. (Courtesy Office of History, 22d Air Refueling Wing.)

While several McConnell Air Force Base tankers and about 200 personnel deployed in support of Operation Desert Storm, all heavy bombing in the war was conducted by Boeing-built B-52s to include these pictured at the time. A U.S. Air Force–wide grounding of the B-1 fleet prevented the jets from deploying to the fight. (Courtesy Department of Defense.)

Senior leaders are not serious, nose-to-the-grindstone people all the time. As this photograph indicates, sometimes they can let loose a little. This photograph shows 384 BMW commander Col. Edgar Ott (right) and the wing vice commander Col. Charlie Brown not-so-gracefully cutting loose, to the amusement of their airmen and a videographer at a base cookout likely in the summer of 1992. Ott was the penultimate commander of the bomb wing at McConnell Air Force Base. (Courtesy Office of History, 22d Air Refueling Wing.)

A historic event that occurred in 1992 was a visit from the Russian Pres. Boris Yeltsin. He came to Kansas primarily to overlook American wheat farming and discuss international trade. This photograph marks his arrival at McConnell Air Force Base at the beginning of his tour on June 18. Yeltsin is in the light suit at left, Wichita mayor Bob Knight is center, and Sen. Bob Dole (R-KS) is at right turning away from the camera. (Courtesy Office of History, 22d Air Refueling Wing.)

Another era comes to a close. On January 4, 1994, the 384 BMW inactivated in a ceremony at McConnell Air Force Base. The actual inactivation was effective on January 1, but the ceremony occurred a few days later to account for the New Year's holiday. In this photograph 384 BMW commander Brig. Gen. Ron Henderson (right) cases his furled colors. A new mission started that same day and McConnell Air Force Base's transformation to the modern era was underway. (Courtesy Office of History, 22d Air Refueling Wing.)

Four

The Modern Era 1994–2008

The collapse of the Soviet Union and lessons learned from Operation Desert Storm led to changes in how the armed forces postured themselves for future operations. As the sole remaining super power in the world, the United States needed a mobile service. The notion of a large number of fixed overseas bases became a thing of the past. For the U.S. Air Force, the driving doctrine was labeled Global Reach. In other words, the U.S. Air Force needed to be able to reach anywhere around the globe on a moments notice, preferably from domestic bases.

This posture change affected the mission of McConnell Air Force Base. With Operation Desert Storm barely in the rear view, McConnell Air Force Base experienced another mission change, as it became one of three "Core Tanker" bases in the U.S. Air Force, alongside Grand Forks Air Force Base in South Dakota and Fairchild out in Washington state. The 22 ARW began operations locally in 1994.

This also created an impact on the 184th Fighter Group. The U.S. Air Force looked to consolidate its B-1 bomber assets at key locations as well. This consolidation resulted in the 184th Fighter Group becoming a B-1B unit. Since its inception, the 184th Fighter Group had known nothing but fighter and pursuit aircraft. From P/F-51 Mustangs in the 1940s to the F-16s they flew in the early 1990s, the 184th was a fighter unit to the core. Now they would transfer to heavies. They became the 184th Bombardment Group in 1994 just as the active duty moved into the tanker realm. This remained the situation until the close of the 20th century.

One more change occurred with the arrival of the 931st Air Refueling Group. This Air Force Reserve unit was attached to the 22 ARW as an associate reserve unit. Shortly thereafter, a big buzzword in U.S. Air Force circles became the term "Total Force," meaning that all air components at a single base be intertwined in a theoretically seamless operation. The 184th Bombardment Wing changed missions again and became a tanker unit in 2002. This remained the case only briefly. Base realignment actions in 2004 changed the 184th Air Refueling Wing yet again. In 2008, the unit became a non-flying intelligence wing. Today "Team McConnell" functions in just such a manner: three independent, yet interdependent, units that contribute to national defense.

Seen here is the first aerial refueling accomplished by the Army Air Service. Lts. Lowell H. Smith and John P. Richter, flying in the lower DeHavilland DH-4, are refueled by the DH-4 tanker flying above them. This event took place in August 1923. Not only was aerial refueling viable technology 70 years later, but it had advanced to the point that U.S. Air Force war fighting doctrine was predicated in part on air-to-air refueling as the means to get to the fight. (Courtesy Air Force Historical Research Agency).

Yet another evolution in the life of McConnell Air Force Base occurred with activation of the 22 ARW and a change of command as well on January 4, 1994. The wing activated, and Brig. Gen. Charles Coolidge took command from then Col. Stephen Loring. This photograph shows Coolidge at center, accepting the wing's colors from Lt. Gen. Walter Kross, 15th U.S. Air Force commander. Colonel Loring stands at right, behind Coolidge. (Courtesy Office of History, 22d Air Refueling Wing.)

One of the first tasks on hand was the continuing rebuild following the 1991 tornado. The multi-year effort was also a modernization project. This photograph shows the construction of Taylor Hall in the mid-1990s. The structure was named for Senior Airman Jeremy Taylor of Rose Hill Kansas who lost his life in the bombing of Khobar Towers in 1996. (Courtesy Office of History, 22d Air Refueling Wing.)

One of the hallmarks of growth in the enlisted force is Professional Military Education. In the 1990s, the Airman Leadership School (ALS) underwent significant development. The photograph at left shows an enlisted volunteer hanging photographs and biographies of airmen who held the Office of the Chief Master Sergeant of the Air Force at the ALS's first permanent home, in the former family center at the now-closed alert facility. The photograph below depicts a distinguished visitor walk through of the new education center at what was then Emerald City, the final home for the ALS. (Courtesy Office of History, 22d Air Refueling Wing.)

The year 1994 brought a new mission and new reality to the 184th as well as the active duty. First the Air Guard unit elevated from group to wing status. Second, for the first time in their 50-plus years of existence, they were no longer flying fighters. In this photograph, an Air Guardsmen goes through a pre-flight check on a B-1B. (Courtesy 184th Intelligence Wing Public Affairs).

An unsurprising site when a base hosts a core tanker wing is a lot of KC-135s. This interesting photograph shows a seemingly never-ending line of Stratotankers, all undergoing changes in tail flashes as they arrive. All were to be converted to the "Keeper of the Plains" flash utilized at McConnell Air Force Base until Air Mobility Command standardized them with base names in 2002. (Courtesy Office of History, 22d Air Refueling Wing.)

The "openness" that came first with Glasnost under Mikhail Gorbechev exploded under Boris Yeltsin when the Russian Republic sprung up. Joint training became an en vogue phenomenon for a brief period. This group of soldiers of the 27th Guard Motorized Rifle Division of the Russian Army landed at McConnell Air Force Base in 1995 to take part in exercises at Fort Riley. (Courtesy Office of History, 22d Air Refueling Wing.)

The Russians were not the only ones "invading" McConnell Air Force Base in 1995. The 931st Air Refueling Group (ARG) also arrived as an associate reserve unit attached to the 22 ARW. The 931 ARG's home unit is the 507th Wing at Tinker Air Force Base, Oklahoma. In this photograph, boom operator SMSgt. John Hallman from the 18th Air Refueling Squadron works out details on his fuel load. (Courtesy Office of History, 931st Air Refueling Group).

A new feature to the old tanker is something known as multi-point air refueling. Utilizing wing pylons with drogue baskets as well as the boom, a KC-135 is capable of refueling any type of aircraft to include helicopters or as in this mid-1990s photograph, Navy F-14 Tomcats. (Courtesy Office of History, 931st Air Refueling Group.)

As in the past, distinguished visitors were a frequent occurrence. Two notable U.S. Air Force leaders passed through McConnell Air Force Base during the 1990s. Gen. Charles Horner, the architect of the air war in Operation Desert Storm, is greeted in the photograph above by then-22 ARW vice commander Col. Ernie Felts, while the photograph below shows Col. Ed Mcilhenny greeting Gen. Richard Myers. Centered between the two is Col. Fred Roggero, then-22 ARW commander. Both Roggero and Mcilhenny would rise to the general officer ranks themselves. (Courtesy Office of History, 22d Air Refueling Wing.)

Though change was common throughout the history of McConnell Air Force Base, one structure remained largely unaffected save for a little remodeling. The base chapel stands now as it did when first opened in 1952. The Chaplain's Corps still sees to the spiritual needs of the armed forces just as they did in the days of George Washington's Continental Army. (Courtesy Office of History, 22d Air Refueling Wing.)

Since integration of the military in 1948, multi-cultural demographics are common on every base in the U.S. Air Force. In fact, the U.S. Air Force was the first of all the service branches to achieve full integration. Today the U.S. Air Force features a wide variety of races and ethnicities. Airman First Class Fredy Pasco was typical of this. The photograph at right, dating from roughly 2000, shows this airman of Peruvian descent playing a native flute. (Courtesy 22d Air Refueling Wing Public Affairs.)

Shown here in a photograph from her days as an All-American at the Air Force Academy, Col. Michelle D. Johnson took command of the 22 ARW on June 14, 2002. A Rhodes Scholar and former presidential aide to both George H. W. Bush and Bill Clinton, Johnson set a McConnell Air Force Base precedent as the first woman to ever command a wing at the base. She also set a U.S. Air Force first as the first woman to command an air refueling wing. Johnson went on to move into the general officer ranks. (Courtesy Headquarters Air Force Public Affairs.)

When Johnson's tour of command ended she was replaced by another woman well-suited to the job. Col. Cathy Clothier started her third tour at McConnell Air Force Base on June 24, 2004. This photograph depicts her change of command ceremony. Johnson is at the right, Clothier at center and presiding officer Maj. Gen. James A. Hawkins, 15th Air Force commander, at left. Clothier was also selected and confirmed for a general's star. (Courtesy Office of History, 22d Air Refueling Wing.)

A maintainer's work is never done. This is especially true when working on nearly 50-year-old aircraft like the KC-135. In the photograph above, an aircraft maintenance technician works on an air refueling boom while SSgt. Alisha Hutcheson replaces a fan blade in an engine intake. Maintenance personnel work round the clock every day of the year to ensure the KC-135 fleet is combat ready. (Courtesy Office of History 22d Air Refueling Wing.)

Throughout the history of McConnell Air Force Base, the military and the city of Wichita have maintained close ties. Both benefit from a partnership that is renowned around the U.S. Air Force. The photograph above, taken at the 2006 open house, shows then-22 ARW commander Col. Donald J. Halpin touring the displays and venues with Mayor Carlos Mayans of Wichita. In the photograph below, from the 2007 Air Force Ball, former 22 ARW commander and now Maj. Gen. Fred Roggero (left) presented the prestigious Fisher Award to three of McConnell Air Force Base's Golden Eagles. From left to right, Jack Pulley, Bob Dool, and Keith Lesher accepted the award on behalf of the Friends of McConnell. The Fisher Award is presented annually to any civic group or organization that demonstrates outstanding support to the armed forces. (Courtesy 22d Air Refueling Wing Public Affairs.)

The worst aviation accident in Wichita history occurred January 16, 1965, when a KC-135 crashed near Piatt and Twenty-first Streets. Thirty people died including the seven-man crew. The top photograph shows the crash site as fire/rescue personnel carry a victim out. The bottom photograph shows Erma Starnes-Winter, a relative of some victims, with the Platt Street Memorial when it was dedicated in the McConnell Airpark on June 9, 2001. (Courtesy Office of History, 22d Air Refueling Wing.)

Team McConnell received a high profile visitor in the fall of 2004. Chief of Staff T. Michael Moseley arrived for a base visit to apprise himself of the scope of operations at McConnell Air Force Base and gain a perspective of the "Total Force" mission there. Such visits while welcome can certainly disrupt routine activity. Rank and file military personnel have long referred to them as "dog and pony shows." (Courtesy Office of History, 22d Air Refueling Wing.)

Like the guard and active duty, the reserves often found themselves subject to visitors as well. Chief of the Air Force Reserve Lt. Gen. John A. Bradley is greeted by 931 ARG commander Col. Tim Cahoun in this 2007 photograph. Bradley was performing a unit visit to get a perception of how operations were going. (Courtesy Office of History, 931st Air Refueling Group.)

Sometimes visits can be pleasant. In 2004, Col. Michelle Johnson welcomed actress Kirstie Alley back to McConnell Air Force Base. During her teen years, Alley worked as a lifeguard at the NCO club pool on McConnell Air Force Base. Alley was a Wichita native who continues to maintain a residence in the city. In the photograph above, Alley is getting a tour of a maintenance hangar. In the photograph at right, Johnson presented her with a memento; a mock up of a KC-135 tail flash.

The 931 ARG achieved a notable first for any refueling unit when one of their crews performed the first-ever refueling of the F-22 Raptor, the U.S. Air Force's newest and most state-of-the-art fighter. The mission occurred on January 21, 2006, and made news across the U.S. Air Force. This photograph shows a view of the Raptor from the window of the boom pod. Technical Sergeant Chris Norris of the 18th Air Refueling Squadron (ARS) conducted the refueling. (Courtesy Office of History, 931st Air Refueling Group.)

By the late 1990s, most construction projects to replace buildings and services destroyed by the 1991 tornado or replace worn down structures was completed. On October 29, 2004, Sen. Robert Dole (R-KS) was honored for securing construction funds. The U.S. Air Force renamed the community center in his honor. Here Dole, 22 ARW vice commander Col. David Kramer, and Rep. Todd Tiahrt (R-KS) unveil the monument in front of the building. (Courtesy Office of History, 22d Air Refueling Wing.)

Proving ingenuity has no rank preference, one NCO with a good idea fundamentally changed the way explosive ordinance disposal teams (EOD) responded to emergencies. In 2004, SSgt. Philip Hauser wrote his idea for a response truck on a napkin. It became the standard EOD response vehicle for the U.S. Air Force. Here he poses with the truck he thought up. (Courtesy Office of History, McConnell Air Force Base.)

This photograph from 2003 provides an interesting view of air refueling from the receiving pilot's perspective. Here a 22 ARW tanker is refueling an F-16 Fighting Falcon. The clear view of the boom's unit markings makes it quite clear just how close these planes get to one another. (Courtesy Office of History, 22d Air Refueling Wing.)

From 1998 until 2003, the Republic of Singapore Air Force maintained a 300-person detachment at McConnell Air Force Base. The Republic of Singapore purchased some surplus KC-135 Stratotankers and the "Peace Guardian" detachment trained with the 350 ARS to train on air refueling techniques, tactics, and general airmanship. This 2003 photograph shows a portion of the detachment's leadership. (Courtesy Office of History, 22d Air Refueling Wing.)

In 2004, the 384 ARS celebrated the Award of the Spaatz Trophy as best air refueling squadron in the U.S. Air Force. The squadron is pictured here after receiving the trophy from Maj. Gen. James Hawkins, 15th Air Force commander standing at far left. Also in the photograph in civilian clothes at center is Keith Lesher, then the squadron's honorary commander and now a McConnell Golden Eagle. (Courtesy Office of History, 22d Air Refueling Wing.)

Arms reduction treaties made treaty compliance a way of life for domestic and foreign military installations. From the late 1990s, McConnell Air Force Base has been subject to compliance inspections under the Strategic Arms Reduction Treaty, or START. These photographs document one such inspection that took place in 2001. In the photograph at right, 22 ARW commander Col. Fred Roggero speaks to the multi-national inspection team. In the photograph below, Col. Ed Flora, 184 BMW commander, presents a Flying Jayhawks ball cap to one of the inspectors. Like Roggero, Flora went on to receive general's stars. (Courtesy Office of History, 22d Air Refueling Wing.)

The tragedy of September 11, 2001, forever changed how America looks at the world and plunged the military into conflicts that have been ongoing ever since. Team McConnell now is fully expeditionary, with a percentage of base personnel deployed everyday of the year, most in Southwest Asia. This photograph from 2003 shows SSgt. Travis Davis on deployment to Bahrain during Operation Iraqi Freedom. Behind him in the background is the water of the Persian Gulf. (Courtesy Office of History, 22d Air Refueling Wing.)

Though war is serious business, people will look for enjoyment wherever they can find it. Here Senior Airman Sarah Harris, an aeromedical technician, and an Airman First Class Salas, an operations support technician, managed to enjoy some fun at a party in the mess tent somewhere in Southwest Asia. (Courtesy Office of History, 22d Air Refueling Wing.)

Occasionally war brings everyday GIs in contact with people of international prominence. In 2004, a member of the 22d Security Forces Squadron's Phoenix Raven Team, Senior Airman Carissa Foy met Pres. Hamid Karzai of Afghanistan. The Phoenix Ravens were airborne security forces that defended aircraft landing at dangerous airstrips that possessed little to no security. (Courtesy Office of History, 22d Air Refueling Wing.)

It is not only the rank-and-file airmen who deploy to the fight. In 2005, 22 ARW commander Col. Cathy Clothier deployed as well to the Combined Air Operations Center. While there, her job took her to places around the theater where she often ran into her own deployed troops. This photograph shows Clothier and a large contingent of Team McConnell people from several squadrons at a location in Southwest Asia. (Courtesy Office of History, 22d Air Refueling Wing.)

Deployment to the war zone was not, and is not, limited merely to combat troops. Support personnel also deploy. In particular need are those that provide tangible products that aid commanders. Photographers such as MSgt. Maurice Hessell documented activities of personnel in the field and recorded photographic records. This photograph from 2006 depicts Hessell plying his trade somewhere in Iraq. (Courtesy Office of History, 22d Air Refueling Wing.)

Inevitably just as deployments have beginnings they also come to an end. Senior Airman Thomas Oullette is shown in this 2003 photograph just after he returned from a base in Southwest Asia. Long distance tanker flights to places like the Persian Gulf region are multiple day affairs, cramped and fatiguing. Oullette's expression and that of the young airman directly behind him clearly illustrate this point. (Courtesy Office of History, 22d Air Refueling Wing.)

With the passage of the Patriot Act, September 11 is forever Patriot's Day. Team McConnell marks this event every year with a ceremony. In this photograph, the gun salute was rendered by a 105 millimeter Howitzer from the 89th Regional Support Command of the U.S. Army Reserve at the 2003 ceremony. (Courtesy Office of History, 22d Air Refueling Wing.)

Showing one's patriotic feelings regained popularity in the public at large since the September 11 attacks; often, military units are key to civilian celebration of such feelings. Such was the case on December 2, 2006, when students from Beech Elementary School took part in the annual "World's Largest Concert." The kids sang "My Country 'Tis of Thee" against a backdrop of military vehicles, aircraft, and the McConnell Air Force Base Honor Guard. The performance was carried by PBS and Armed Forces Television. (Courtesy 22d Air Refueling Wing Public Affairs.)

McConnell Air Force Base personnel continued their training cycles in spite of ongoing activities in other parts of the world. Generation exercises demand much of operations and maintenance. Their overall purpose is to launch as many aircraft in as short a time as possible to train for and evaluate a wing's ability to get out of town. One such exercise in the spring of 2006 produced the result shown here as a multitude of KC-135s taxi to launch in short intervals of about 15–20 seconds between jet launch. (Courtesy Office of History, 22d Air Refueling Wing.)

Previous and current operations did not stop other routine activity either. McConnell Air Force Base units have continuously deployed personnel since Operation Desert Shield in 1990. This photograph from the late 1990s shows the color guard preparing to perform a detail likely involving the posting of the colors. (Courtesy Office of History, 22d Air Refueling Wing.)

This is Easter time on an air base. Children of military families partake in a time-honored base tradition in the spring of 2008 by taking part in an Easter egg hunt in the family housing area. For decades, military installations have marked major holidays both religious and secular as they come round. McConnell Air Force Base has never been different in that regard as the illustration clearly shows. (Courtesy 22d Air Refueling Wing, Public Affairs.)

A true role model meets with admirers. Maj. Nicole Malachowski was the first female pilot in the history of the Thunderbirds, one of whose founding members hailed from Derby. Major Malachowski flew the No. 3 jet for the team during her tour with them. Here at McConnell Air Force Base's 2006 Air Show, a young admirer received a face-to-face meeting she will likely never forget. (Courtesy Office of History, 22d Air Refueling Wing.)

The active duty are not the only military members who deploy. The National Guard and, as shown in this photograph, the Reserves do as well. Likely taken in 2007, members of the 931st ARG off-load bags of personnel who just returned to McConnell Air Force Base aboard a reserve KC-135 from Grissom Air Force Base in Indiana. The airmen are utilizing the time honored "bucket brigade" method. Unlike modern U.S. Air Force cargo jets such as the C-17, the venerable KC-135 does not possess ramps to on load or off load cargo. Baggage is almost always manually loaded and unloaded. (Courtesy Office of History, 931st Air Refueling Group.)

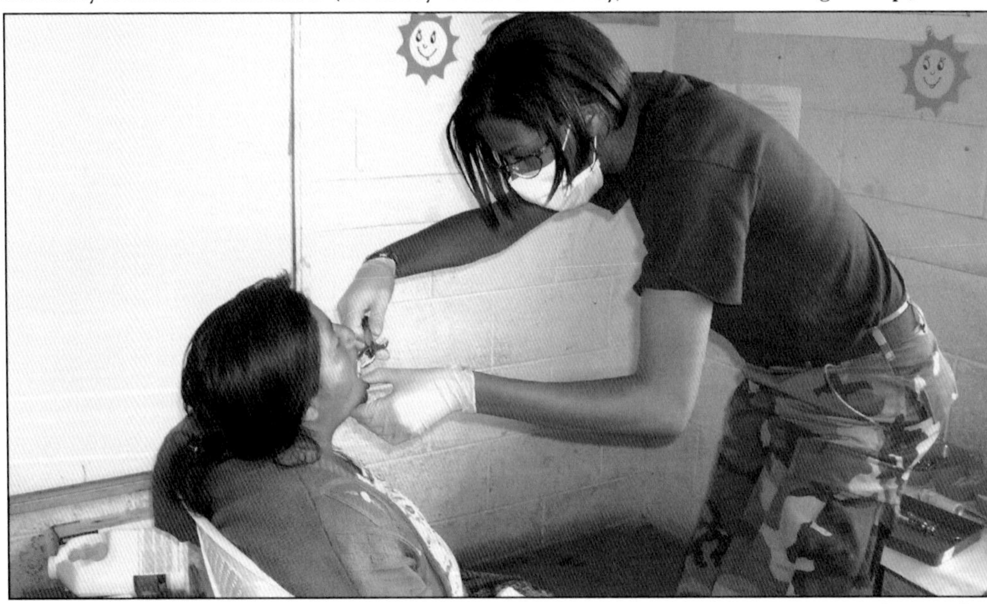

Not all deployments are centered on war fighting. Military members also perform something called "operations other than war," or OOTW. One recent OOTW mission performed by personnel of the 931st took them to Guatemala in 2007. This photograph shows a dental technician from the 931st Aeromedical Flight performing a procedure on a patient. The medics are often tasked with such humanitarian missions. (Courtesy Office of History, 931st Air Refueling Group.)

A sign of the post 9-11 era was a change to medical response capabilities. These photographs, both above and below, show the 22d Medical Group's new joint biological agent identification and diagnostic system, or JBAIDS for short, acquired in 2007. The trailer is designed for transport to emergency sites so laboratory technicians can perform real-time biological agent analysis. JBAIDS came into being as a result of some of the anthrax scares in the months and years following the 9-11 attacks. The photograph above shows the trailer exterior, and the photograph below shows some of the equipment utilized by lab technicians. (Courtesy 22d Air Refueling Wing Public Affairs.)

McConnell Air Force Base developed its own combat skills training area on the southeast side of the base that allows personnel to run through various scenarios in order to gain exposure to simulated combat operations. In this 2007 photograph, 22 ARW commander Col. Donald Halpin pours water down the back of Airman First Class Krystal Barron of the 22d Logistics Readiness Squadron to cool her off. (Courtesy 22d Air Refueling Wing Public Affairs.)

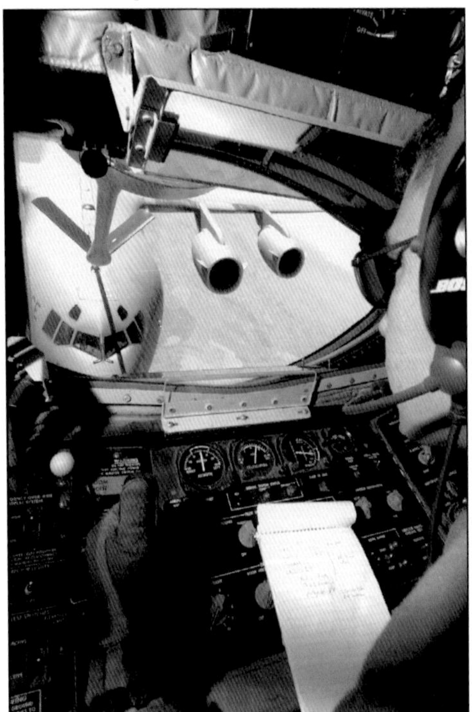

A more modern competition, born out of the old SAC Bomb-Nav contest, is the AMC (Air Mobility Command) Rodeo. Crews validate their training and proficiency through a number of tests. Those who scored best took home the trophies. Here boom operator Technical Sergeant Matthew Calisi refuels a KC-135RT at the 2007 rodeo. Eight RT models exist in the U.S. Air Force and all are based at McConnell Air Force Base. They are the only KC-135s that can be refueled in air. (Courtesy Office of History, 22d Air Refueling Wing.)

Following a devastating tornado in Greensburg in 2007, Pres. George W. Bush arrived to visit the area. This photograph shows Bush's arrival at McConnell Air Force Base. Elected officials, especially high-ranking visitors, will often use military bases as a matter of logistics given the ample communications, maintenance, and supply support. This May 9, 2007, photograph shows Bush deplaning *Air Force One* along with Sen. Sam Brownback (middle) and Sen. Pat Roberts trailing Brownback. (Courtesy 22d Air Refueling Wing Public Affairs.)

President Bush was greeted by 22 ARW vice commander Col. John Zazworsky upon his departure on June 15, 2007. The governor of Kansas Kathleen Sebelius also accompanied Bush, Brownback, and Roberts for the trip to Greensburg. The tornado literally destroyed 95 percent of the small farming community. (Courtesy 22d Air Refueling Wing Public Affairs.)

More change comes to the 184th. In October 2007, the 184th began another mission transition as the unit's evolution from tanker wing to intelligence wing got underway with the activation of the 161st Intelligence Squadron. Marking the occasion among other were Gov. Kathleen Sebelius (fourth from left), Sen. Sam Brownback (second from left), Sen. Pat Roberts (third from right), Brig. Gen. Ed McIlhenny (second from right), and Rep. Todd Tiahrt (right). (Courtesy 22d Air Refueling Wing Public Affairs.)

The September 2007 Air Force Ball arguably brought the McConnell Air Force Base community their highest profile keynote speaker in base history when L. Paul Bremer, the first ambassador in charge of the Coalition Provisional Authority in Iraq after the fall of Saddam Hussein, spoke to the gathered guests. His address dealt largely with his actions and decisions during his tenure. (Courtesy 22d Air Refueling Wing Public Affairs.)

The paradox of military service is represented in these two photographs. In the photograph at right, Technical Sergeant James Caughron of the 22d Civil Engineering Squadron was selected as of 1 of the U.S. Air Force's 12 "Outstanding Airmen" for 2008, and justifiably so. The photograph below shows Chief Master Sergeant John Gephardt cradling a wounded Iraqi girl at Balad Air Base, Iraq. The photograph created a national sensation when it went public in 2007. Both men took their respective notoriety in stride. Therein laid the paradox; accolades responded to with humble reaction. (Courtesy Office of History, 22d Air Refueling Wing.)

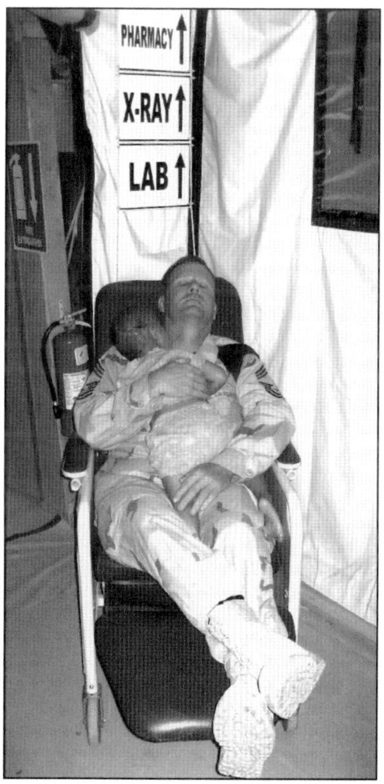

Fitness is the new view in the U.S. Air Force that now goes outside the base and more frequently than ever finds its airmen engaging in ground combat. Competitions such as the 2005 Combat Triathlon tested the mettle of McConnell Air Force Base airmen. Here Chief Master Sergeant James McDowell (right) leads his team on a full-pack, double-time march along the road to their next competition venue. (Courtesy Office of History, 22d Air Refueling Wing.)

In the military, change is common and always occurring. That includes with the leadership as well. Col. James C. Vechery (right) took command of the 22 ARW from Maj. Gen. James Hawkins on February 8, 2008. In this photograph, Vechery accepts the colors of his new wing, adorned with it awards and battle streamers that date back to the beginning of America's involvement in World War II. (Courtesy 22d Air Refueling Wing Public Affairs.)

The Tops In Blue performance troupe exhibits the many talents of U.S. Air Force personnel when it both domestically and internationally entertains in war zones and at places like the Cotillion in Wichita as they did in this early 2008 photograph. The group routinely performs in civilian venues and in many cases exposes the general public to a side of the U.S. Air Force they will not see on CNN. (Courtesy 22d Air Refueling Wing Public Affairs.)

BIBLIOGRAPHY

Bednarek, Janet R. *Generations of Chevrons: An Enlisted History Through the Experiences of the Chief Master Sergeants of the Air Force*. Washington, D.C.: Air Force History and Museums Program, 2004.

Knaack, Marcelle Size. *Post World War II Bombers*. Washington, D.C.: Office of Air Force History, 1988.

Larsen, Steve A. *Heritage and Legacy: A Brief History of the 22d Air Refueling Wing and McConnell Air Force Base*. McConnell Air Force Base: Office of History, 22d Air Refueling Wing, 2006.

Nalty, Bernard C. *Winged Shield and Winged Sword: A History of the United States Air Force*, 2 Vols. Washington, D.C.: Air Force History and Museums Program, 1997.

Price, Maj. James, *Kansas Air National Guard: 1941–2004*. Marceline, MO: Walsworth Publishing, 2007.

Price, Jay M., *Wichita's Legacy of Flight*. Charleston, SC: Arcadia Publishing, 2003.

Rowe, Frank Joseph and Miner, Craig. *Borne on the South Wind*. Wichita, KS: Wichita Eagle and Beacon Publishing, 1994.

Shaw, Frederick J., editor. *Locating Air Force Base Sites: History's Legacy*. Washington, D.C.: Air Force History and Museums Program, 2004.

Stumpf, David K. *Titan II: A History of a Cold War Missile Program*. Fayetteville, AR: University of Arkansas Press, 2000.

Thompson, Susan. *Prairie Runways: The History of Wichita's Original Municipal Airport*. Wichita, KS: Air Capital Press, 2000.